GW00702310

Death

by
Shaikh 'Alee Hasan 'Alee 'Abdul-Hameed

translated by
Aboo Talhah Daawood ibn Ronald Burbank

ISBN 1 898649 06 5

British Library Cataloguing in Publication Data.

A catalogue record for this book is available from the British Library.

First Edition, 1415 AH/1994 CE

© Copyright 1994 by Al-Hidaayah Publishing & Distribution

*All rights reserved. No part of this publi-
cation may be reproduced in any language,
stored in a retrieval system or transmitted
in any form or by any means, electronic,
mechanical, photocopying, recording or oth-
erwise without the express permission of
the copyright owner.*

Cover design: Prem Karra

Typeset by: Al-Hidaayah Publishing & Distribution

Published by: Al-Hidaayah Publishing & Distribution
                   P.O. Box 3332
                   Birmingham
                   United Kingdom
                   B10 0UH

                   Tel: 0121 753 1889
                   Fax: 0121 753 2422

Email: mail@al-hidaayah.co.uk

بِسْمِ اللَّهِ الرَّحْمَٰنِ الرَّحِيمِ

قُلْ هَٰذِهِ سَبِيلِي أَدْعُو إِلَى اللَّهِ عَلَىٰ بَصِيرَةٍ أَنَا وَمَنِ اتَّبَعَنِي وَسُبْحَانَ اللَّهِ وَمَا أَنَا مِنَ الْمُشْرِكِينَ ﴿١٠٨﴾

Say (O Muhammad): This is my way; I invite unto Allaah with sure knowledge, I and whosoever follows me (also must invite others to Allaah) with sure knowledge. And Glorified and Exalted be Allaah (above all that they associate as partners with Him). And I am not of the polytheists.

Soorah Yoosuf (12):108

بِسْمِ اللّٰهِ الرَّحْمٰنِ الرَّحِيْمِ

يَاأَيُّهَا الَّذِينَ آمَنُوا لَا تُلْهِكُمْ أَمْوَالُكُمْ وَلَا أَوْلَادُكُمْ عَن ذِكْرِ اللَّهِ وَمَن يَفْعَلْ ذَٰلِكَ فَأُولَٰئِكَ هُمُ الْخَاسِرُونَ ۝ وَأَنفِقُوا مِن مَّا رَزَقْنَاكُم مِّن قَبْلِ أَن يَأْتِيَ أَحَدَكُمُ الْمَوْتُ فَيَقُولَ رَبِّ لَوْلَا أَخَّرْتَنِي إِلَىٰ أَجَلٍ قَرِيبٍ فَأَصَّدَّقَ وَأَكُن مِّنَ الصَّالِحِينَ ۝ وَلَن يُؤَخِّرَ اللَّهُ نَفْسًا إِذَا جَاءَ أَجَلُهَا وَاللَّهُ خَبِيرٌ بِمَا تَعْمَلُونَ ۝

O you who believe! Let not your properties nor your children divert you from the remembrance of Allaah. Whosoever does that, then they are the losers. So spend (in charity) of that with which We have provided you, before death comes to one of you and he says: "My Lord! If only You would give me respite for a little while (i.e. return to the worldly life), then I should give Sadaqah (i.e. Zakat - obligatory charity) of my wealth, and be among the righteous." But Allaah grants respite to none when his appointed time (death) comes. And Allaah is All-Aware of what you do.

Soorah al-Munaafiqoon (63):9-11

The Messenger of Allaah (ﷺ) said: "Remember much that which cuts off pleasures: Death. Since no one remembers it in times of difficulty except that things are made easy for him, nor mentions it at times of ease except that the affairs become constricted for him."

Saheehul-Jaami'us-Sagheer, no.1222

CONTENTS

بِسْمِ اللَّهِ الرَّحْمَٰنِ الرَّحِيمِ

Introduction

All praise is for Allaah. We praise Him, seek His aid and ask for His forgiveness. We seek Allaah's refuge from the evils of ourselves and from our evil actions. Whomsoever Allaah guides then none can misguide him, and whomsoever Allaah misguides then none can guide him. I testify that none has the right to be worshipped but Allaah alone, having no partners, and I testify that Muhammad is His Slave and Messenger.

To proceed:

Before you, O Muslim, is a small treatise containing noble *Aayaat* of the Qur'aan, authentic sayings of the Prophet (ﷺ) and selected *Sharee'ah* rulings.

Despite its small size, it comprises of that which the Muslim should know about death, the admonition it provides us with, and the encouragements and warnings related to it, as well as its effect upon the life of the Muslim.

It contains an abridgement of much of what is reported in the Book of Allaah, the One free and far removed form all defects and the Most High, and what is authentically reported from the *Sunnah* of Allaah's Messenger (ﷺ) - with regard to Islamic regulations about funerals and related matters, whilst explaining the correct view where there is a difference of opinion amongst the scholars. These rulings are quoted without mentioning the evidences, discussion of the topic or quotations of the details from the books of *fiqh*, in order to make the book easy to read and to avoid making it lengthy.[4]

---

[4] All this is abridged from the beautiful book of our teacher Shaykh Al-Albaanee entitled, *Ahkaamul-Janaa'iz*, after revision and ordering, so whoever wishes to know the evidences then let him refer to that.

The aim of this treatise is to make it easy to refer to the *fiqh* regulations concerning funerals when death occurs, which is something inevitable whether sooner or later, since it is a fact that the books written about this - being excellent but large - are difficult to refer to for the common Muslim, and even for the educated or the student of knowledge, particularly when the misfortune strikes and the hearts are preoccupied!

Finally, I ask Allaah, the Most Great, that He directs all the Muslims to the following of the Book of Allaah, He the One far removed and free from all defects, and the *Sunnah* of Allaah's Messenger (ﷺ) in all affairs in their lives, indeed He is the Hearing, and the One Who responds. And our final call is that all praise is for Allaah, Lord of the Worlds.

'Alee Hasan 'Alee 'Abdul-Hameed

Chapter I

Admonition

A Reminder

Death is a harsh and fearful reality faced by everyone who lives. No one has the power to avoid it, nor does anyone around the dying person have the ability to prevent it. It is something which happens every moment and is encountered by the old and the young, the rich and the poor, the strong and the weak. They are all the same in that they have no plan or means of escaping it, no power, no means of intercession, no way to prevent it, nor to delay it, which shows that indeed it comes from one having tremendous power - so that the human is helpless in this regard and can only submit to it.

So in Allaah's Hand alone is the granting of life, and in His Hand is the return of what He gave at the appointed time, and after the allotted life span, whether the people are in their houses amongst their families, or striving to seek provision or striving for 'aqeedah (correct belief). Reward and recompense are with Him, and He has full knowledge and power.

So the return of all is to Allaah, and they will be raised up before Allaah, having no place of return except that, and no destiny but this one. So they will differ from one another only due to their deeds and intentions, and according to the way they followed and their seriousness in that. But with regard to their end, then it is one, death at the appointed time, after the decreed span, and then the return to Allaah and resurrection on the Day of Gathering of mankind. Then Forgiveness and Mercy from Allaah, or His Anger and His Punishment.

So the greatest fool is the one who chooses the wretched fate, and he is certain to die whatever happens:

Everyone shall taste death...[5]

This reality must be established firmly in ones heart, the reality that life in this world is limited and has an appointed end - and this end will definitely come...

The righteous will die and the wicked will die...
The warriors who fight Jihaad will die and those who sit at home will die...
Those who busy themselves with correct belief will die and those who treat the people as their slaves will die...
The brave who reject injustice will die, and the cowards who seek to cling on to this life at any price will die...
The people of great concern and lofty goals will die,
and the wretched people who live only for cheap enjoyment will die...

All will die:

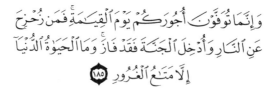

Everyone shall taste death...[6]

Everyone's soul will taste it and will depart from this life. There will be no difference between one soul and another in tasting from this cup which passes between them all, rather the difference is in something else. The difference is in the place of their destination:

$$وَإِنَّمَا تُوَفَّوْنَ أُجُورَكُمْ يَوْمَ ٱلْقِيَـٰمَةِ ۖ فَمَن زُحْزِحَ عَنِ ٱلنَّارِ وَأُدْخِلَ ٱلْجَنَّةَ فَقَدْ فَازَ ۗ وَمَا ٱلْحَيَوٰةُ ٱلدُّنْيَآ إِلَّا مَتَـٰعُ ٱلْغُرُورِ ﴿١٨٥﴾$$

---

[5] Soorah Aali-'Imraan (3):185

[6] Soorah Aali-'Imraan (3):185

And only on the Day of Resurrection shall you be paid your wages in full. So whoever is removed away from the Fire and admitted to Paradise, he indeed is successful.[7]

This is what is of true worth and is that which will cause the difference between souls, this is the final resting place which will mean separation of one person from another, that which is of true and everlasting value, which deserves to be strived for and that one should exert ones efforts for its attainment, and the other destination is to be dreaded, and it deserves that one should take account of oneself a thousand times...[8]

Noble *Aayaat*

Many Sublime *Aayaat* mention death, from them is the saying of the One free and far removed from all imperfections, and the Most High:

$$﴿وَلَقَدْ كُنتُمْ تَمَنَّوْنَ ٱلْمَوْتَ مِن قَبْلِ أَن تَلْقَوْهُ فَقَدْ رَأَيْتُمُوهُ وَأَنتُمْ تَنظُرُونَ ١٤٣﴾$$

You did indeed wish for death (martyrdom) before you met it. Now you have seen it openly with your own eyes.[9]

His saying:

$$قُلْ إِنَّ ٱلْمَوْتَ ٱلَّذِى تَفِرُّونَ مِنْهُ فَإِنَّهُ مُلَـٰقِيكُمْ ثُمَّ تُرَدُّونَ$$
$$إِلَىٰ عَـٰلِمِ ٱلْغَيْبِ وَٱلشَّهَـٰدَةِ فَيُنَبِّئُكُم بِمَا كُنتُمْ تَعْمَلُونَ ٨$$

Say: "Verily, the death from which you flee will surely meet you, then you will be sent back to (Allaah), the All-Knower of the unseen and the seen, and He will tell you what you used to do."[10]

---

7 Soorah Aali-'Imraan (3):185

8 *Al-Yawmul-Aakhir fee Dhilaalil-Qur'aan*, (pp.59-60), adapted slightly.

9 Soorah Aali-'Imraan (3):143

10 Soorah al-Jumu'ah (62):8

His saying:

And we granted not to any human being immortality before you (O Muhammad (ﷺ)), then if you die, would they live forever? Everyone is going to taste death, and We shall make a trial of you with evil and with good, and to Us you will be returned.[11]

His saying:

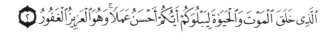

(He) Who has created death and life, that He may test which of you is best in deed. He is the All-Mighty, the Oft-Forgiving.[12]

Prophetic *Ahaadeeth*

The Prophetic *ahaadeeth* reported concerning death and the effect it should have, are many. I will quote a single very important narration from them and suffice with that:

From Al-Baraa' ibn 'Aazib, (*radiyallaahu 'anhumaa*), who said,

"We went out with Allaah's Messenger (ﷺ) with the funeral of a man of the Ansaar and we came to the grave and the niche in the side of the grave (al-Lahd)[13] had not been dug out yet, so Allaah's Messenger (ﷺ)

---

[11] Soorah al-Anbiyaa' (21):34-35

[12] Soorah al-Mulk (67):2

[13] The niche in the side of the grave facing the Qiblah in which the body is placed.

sat and we sat around him as if we had birds upon our heads[14] and in his hand he had a stick with which he was striking the ground. Then he raised his head and said, "Seek Allaah's refuge from the Punishment of the Grave," two or three times. Then he said, "When the Believing servant is leaving this world and going on to the Hereafter, angels with white faces - as if their faces were the sun - descend upon him. With them is a shroud from the shrouds of Paradise and perfume for embalming from the perfume of Paradise, so they sit away from him at the distance the eye can see and then the Angel of Death, *alaihis-salaam*, comes and sits by his head and says, "O good soul, come out to forgiveness from Allaah and His good pleasure." He said, "So it comes out just as a drop flows out from the mouth of the drinking vessel, and he takes it, but does not leave it in his hand even for the blink of an eye until they take it and place it in that shroud and that perfume, and there comes out from him a smell like that of the best musk found upon the face of the earth." He said, " So they ascend with it [i.e. the persons soul] and they do not pass by any group of the angels except that they say, "Who is this good and pure soul?" So they reply, "So and so, son of so and so," with the best of his names which he used to be called by in this world until they come with him to the lowest heaven and ask that it be opened for him, so it is opened for him, so they accompany him through every heaven to the next one until he is taken up to the seventh heaven, and Allaah, the Mighty and Magnificent, says, "Write the record of my slave in *'Illiyyoon*[15] and return to the earth to his body." So then two angels come to him and make him sit up. Then they say, "Who is your Lord?" So he will say, "My Lord is Allaah." So they say, "What is your *Deen?*" So he will say, "My *Deen* is Islaam?" So they say, "Who is this man who was sent amongst you?" So he will say, "He is Allaah's Messenger." So they say, "How did

---

[14] Showing that one should be silent during the burial, and not raise ones voice with *dhikr*, nor shouting out *tahleel* and *takbeer* - so consider!

[15] From the root word *'Uluww* signifying highness, and it is said that it is the seventh heaven where the souls of the believers are to be found.

Publishers Note: See the Qur'aan, Soorah al-Mutaffifeen (83):18-20.

you come to know that?" So he will say, "I read the Book of Allaah, and believed in it and attested to it." So a caller will call from Heaven, "Indeed My servant has spoken the truth, so spread a place for him in Paradise, and open a door to Paradise for him." He said, "So some of its fragrance and scent comes to him and his grave is extended as far as the eye can see." He said, "A person with a handsome face, beautiful clothes and good smell comes to him and says, 'Receive good news which will please you. This is the day which you were promised.'" So he says to him, "Who are you? Since your face appears to signify good." So he says, "I am your righteous actions." He therefore says, "O Lord, establish the Last Hour, O Lord establish the Last Hour - so that I may return to my family and wealth." But when the unbelieving servant is leaving this world and going onto the Hereafter, angels with black faces descend upon him, with them are coarse sack-cloths, and they sit at a distance from him as far as the eye can see. Then the Angel of Death comes and sits by his head and says, "O foul soul, come out to Allaah's displeasure and anger." So (the soul) spreads throughout his body, so he drags it out just as a pronged roasting fork is pulled through wool. So he takes it, but does not leave it in his hand for the blink of an eye until they put it in those coarse sack-cloths. Then there comes from him an offensive stench like that of the foulest smelling corpse rotting upon the face of the earth. So they ascend with it (i.e the soul) and they do not pass by any group of angels except that they say, "What is this foul smell?" So they say, "So and so, son of so and so," calling him with the ugliest names which he used to be called with in this world, until they come with him to the lowest heaven and ask for permission to enter, and it is not opened for him." Then Allaah's Messenger (ﷺ) recited:

لَا تُفَتَّحُ لَهُمْ أَبْوَابُ السَّمَاءِ وَلَا يَدْخُلُونَ الْجَنَّةَ حَتَّىٰ يَلِجَ الْجَمَلُ فِى سَمِّ الْخِيَاطِ

...for them the gates of heaven will not be opened, and they will not enter Paradise until the camel goes through the eye of the needle (which is impossible).[16]

---

[16] Soorah al-A'raaf (7):40

So Allaah, the Mighty and Magnificent, says, "Write his record in 'Sijjeen'[17] within the lowest earth." Then his soul is flung down, and he recited:

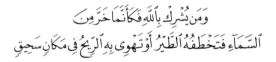

...and whoever assigns partners to Allaah, it is as if he had fallen from the sky, and the birds had snatched him, or the wind had thrown him to a far off place.[18]

So his soul is returned to his body and two Angels come and make him sit up. Then they will say to him, "Who is your Lord?" So he will say, "Ah, ah, I do not know." So they will say to him, "What is your Deen?" So he will say, "Ah, ah, I do not know." So they will say to him, "Who is this man who was sent amongst you?" So he will say, "Ah, ah, I do not know." So a caller will call from heaven, "You have lied so spread a place for him in the Fire, and open a door to the Fire for him." So some of its heat and scorching air comes upon him, and his grave is constricted to the extent that his ribs interlace, and a man with an ugly face, unsightly clothes and smelling offensively comes to him and says, "Receive news of that which will grieve you, this is the day which you were promised." So he will say, "Who are you? Your face is ugly and seems to signify evil." So he will say, "I am your evil actions." So he will say, "O Lord, Do not establish the Last Hour."[19]

---

17 A name signifying constrictedness.

18 Soorah al-Hajj (22):31

19 *Saheehul-Jaami'*, reported by Ahmad and others.

The Unexpected Occurs

A noble person said:

How many people I have known, if I wished, I could name them, who surrendered themselves to their desires and became prisoners of their lusts and forgot about death and their reckoning. So when Allaah, the Mighty and Magnificent guided me to His obedience, to following His orders, and to fearing Him, then I went to my friend, advising him, and admonishing him with encouragement and warning, but he used the excuse that he was still a young man, and he was fooled by false hopes. Then, by Allaah, death came unexpectedly. So now he is one who lies buried under the earth, tied to the burden of his sins. His passions have left him, his female companions have departed from him and now he must face the consequences, now he has to face the Overpowering Compellor with the actions of the sinful and depraved...

May Allaah save you and I from a record or an end like his. So fear Allaah, O Servants of Allaah, and do not be like him, since you know that this world is passing away and the Hereafter is coming towards us, so keep in mind the point of death and one's passing on, and the number of sins that one has committed and the small amount of good that one has done. Think of the good that you would earnestly wish to do at that time - then bring that forward and do that today, and think of all those things which you would desire to clear yourself from, then clear yourself from them now.

"If it were the case that when we die we would be left untroubled,
　　Then death would be rest and relaxation for everyone living:
However when we die we shall be raised up again,
　　And questioned about everything we have done."[20]

---

20 *Ahwaalul-Qiyaamah* (pp.4-5)

Chapter 2

Funeral Regulations

Abridged from the book *Ahkaamul-Janaa'iz* of the scholar Shaykh Muhammad Naasiruddeen al-Albaanee

Regulations for the Sick

(1) He should be contented with what Allaah has predestined, and patiently bear what He has decreed, having good thoughts about his Lord, since it is what is best for him.

(2) He should have both fear and hope. Fearing Allaah's Punishment for his sins and hoping for the Mercy of His Lord.

(3) However serious his illness becomes he may not wish for death, but if it reaches the point that he has to, then he should say:

اللهُمَّ أَحْيِني ما كانَتِ الحَياةُ خَيْراً لي ، وتَوَفَّني إذا كانَتِ الوَفاةُ خَيْراً لي

(*Allaahumma ahyeenee maa kaanatil hayaatu khairallee wa tawaffanee idhaa kaanatil wafaatu khairallee*)

"O Allaah grant me life as long as life is best for me, and cause me to die when death is best for me."

(4) If there are any outstanding debts or rights people have over him then let him settle them with those he owes them to if that is possible for him, and if not then let him write that in his will.[21]

(5) He must hasten to write his will (*al-Wasiyyah*).

---

[21] The text of a will acceptable in the *Sharee'ah* can be found at the end of the book (p.42).

At the Point of Death

(1) When a person is dying then the following should be carried out by those present:

> (a) They should tell him to say, 'Laa ilaaha illallaah' (None has the right to be worshipped except Allaah).
>
> (b) They should supplicate (make du'aa) for him.
>
> (c) They should only say that which is good in his presence.

(2) As for reciting Soorah Yaa-Seen in his presence, and turning him to face the Qiblah, then there is no authentic hadeeth about that at all.

(3) There is no harm in a Muslim being present at the death of an unbeliever, in order to present Islaam to him, hoping that he accepts Islaam.

After Death

(1) When the person dies, and his soul departs, then those present should perform the following:

> (a) Close the eyes of the deceased.
>
> (b) Supplicate for the deceased.
>
> (c) Cover the deceased with a cloth covering the whole body as long as he is not in the state of Ihraam,[22] since in that case his face and head should not be covered.
>
> (d) They should hasten in preparing him for burial and taking him for burial, when they are certain that he is dead.
>
> (e) He should be buried in the land where he died and not moved to another, except for a necessity, since this is contrary to the order to hasten in burying him.
>
> (f) That one or more of them hastens to pay off the deceased's debts from the wealth of the deceased himself, even if it takes up all of his wealth. But if he has no wealth then the State should pay it off for him, if he had himself tried to pay it off. If that is not done,

---

[22] i.e. whilst one is performing the rites of Hajj or 'Umrah. **[Translator's note]**

and one or more persons choose to pay it off for him, then that is allowed.

Permissible Actions for the Close Relatives and Others who are Present

(1) It is permissible for them to uncover the face of the deceased and to kiss him, and to weep for him, without wailing, screaming or tearing the clothes (*Niyaahah*), for three days.

(2) There are two things obligatory upon the relatives of the deceased when the news of the death reaches them:
    (a) To be patient and to be content with Allaah's decree and what He has predestined.
    (b) '*al-Istirjaa*' and that is to say with understanding and reflecting on its meaning:

(*Innaa lillaahi wa innaa ilaihi raaji'oon*)
'Indeed we belong to Allaah, and to Him we will certainly return.'

(3) Bearing with patience does not conflict with a woman's avoiding all adornment, as long as this is for no more than three days, in mourning for her father or other than him. However if the deceased is her husband, then she should mourn for four months and ten days, all this being reported in the texts.

(4) So if the deceased is other than her husband and she does not mourn, in order to please her husband and to allow him to benefit from her as intended - then that is better for her, and it is to be hoped that it will be a source of much good.

What is not Allowed for them

(1) Allaah's Messenger (ﷺ) forbade a number of matters which people used to do, and some still do, when a relative dies. These things must therefore be known, in order to be avoided:

> (a) (*Niyaahah*) - which is what is beyond weeping, and includes wailing and shrieking, striking one's face and tearing clothes etc.
>
> (b) Dishevelling the hair, i.e. causing it to become untidy.
>
> (c) The practice of some men of allowing their beards to grow for a few days in mourning for the deceased, then they return to their former practice of shaving them![23] So this limited keeping of the beard falls under the forbidden practice of dishevelling the hair at this time, and Allaah knows best.
>
> (d) Announcing the death from minarets and the like, since that is from the forbidden means of announcing death.

Announcing the Death in a Permissible Manner

(1) Announcing the death is allowed as long as it is not done in a manner resembling what was done in the time of Ignorance (*Jaahiliyyah*). Indeed announcing the death may sometimes be obligatory, when there is no one present to fulfill the right he has of being washed, shrouded, and having the Funeral Prayer said over him.

(2) It is permissible for the one who informs of the death to ask people to pray for forgiveness for the deceased, since that is reported in the pure Sunnah.[24]

---

[23] Despite the fact that leaving the beard to grow is an obligation and that shaving it is forbidden, as I have explained in my treatise, *Hukmud-Deen fil-Lihyah wat-Tadkheen*.

[24] This *Sunnah* is however contradicted by many people who instead say, 'Read al-Faatihah for the soul of so an so,' or other than this, having no basis in the *Sunnah*!

Signs of a Good End to Ones Life

It is established from the Prophet (ﷺ) that he informed us of a number of clear signs which are an indication that a person has concluded his life upon good, and we ask Allaah, the One free of all imperfections, that He grant us that. So any person who dies in one of these ways then it is glad tidings for them, and how excellent this is:

(1) Pronouncing the *Shahaadah* (*La ilaaha illallaah*) when dying.

(2) Dying with sweat upon the brow.

(3) Dying on the night preceding or the day of Friday.

(4) Martyrdom upon the battlefield.[25]

(5) Death due to plague.

(6) Death due to stomach illness.

(7) Death by drowning.

(8) Death due to a building falling upon him.

(9) Death of a woman during pregnancy due to the child.

(10) Death through consumption/tuberculosis.

(11) Death whilst defending the *Deen* or ones person.

(12) Death whilst defending ones property from robbers.

(13) Death whilst defending the frontiers of Islaam.

(14) Death whilst doing a righteous action.

(15) Death in a fire.

People's Praise of the Deceased

(1) If a group of truthful Muslims speak in praise of the deceased, their number being two or more of the people of piety and knowledge who lived near to and knew the deceased, then Paradise is assured for him.

(2) If a person dies at the time of an eclipse of the sun or moon, then that does not indicate anything. The belief that it shows the importance of the deceased is a false superstition of the times of Ignorance.

---

[25] This martyrdom, may Allaah grant it to us, is to be hoped for by everyone who prays for it sincerely, even if he is not able to die upon the battlefield, as occurs in the authentic *hadeeth*.

Washing the Deceased

(1) After the deceased has passed away it becomes obligatory that some of the people wash his body.

(2) In washing the body the following actions are to be observed:

(a) That the body is washed three times or more than that depending upon the need.

(b) That the body is washed an odd number of times.

(c) That for some of the washing, leaves of the lotus tree be put in the water, or something that will cleanse in its place, soap for example.

(d) That some perfume be mixed with the final washing,[26] preference being given to camphor.

(e) Braids in the hair are to be undone and washed well.

(f) The hair is to be combed.

(g) The woman's hair is then to be made into three braids and placed behind her.

(i) Men should be washed by men, and women by women.[27]

(j) The washing is done using a cloth or its like, and the body is to be covered by a sheet, being stripped of clothing.

(k) The one who should perform the washing is the one who knows best about the *Sunnah* of washing, especially if he is from the family or close relatives of the deceased.

(3) There is a great reward for the one who washes the deceased as long as two conditions are fulfilled:

(a) That he keeps anything that he sees secret and does not disclose anything disagreeable.

---

[26] The exception to this being a person who dies in *ihraam*, since it is not allowed to perfume him.

[27] An exception to this is the husband and wife, since each of them may wash the other since there is no proof to prevent it and in origin it is something permissible and there is in fact support for it in the *Sunnah*.

(b) That he does it seeking thereby Allaah's Face, not seeking reward or thanks from the people, nor anything from this world. Since Allaah does not accept any of the actions done seeking the Hereafter, except those done purely for His Face.

(4) It is recommended (*Mustahabb*) for the one who has washed a dead body to take a bath himself, and it is not an obligation.

(5) It is not prescribed for a martyr who died upon the battlefield to be washed, even if he was in a state of *janaabah* (i.e. required a bath due to sexual intercourse or emission of semen).

Shrouding the Body

(1) After washing the deceased it is obligatory to shroud him.

(2) The shroud or its price is to come from the wealth of the deceased, even if that is the only wealth that he has.

(3) The shroud should cover the whole body.

(4) If it is not possible to obtain a shroud which covers his whole body, then the head downwards should be covered, and any part left uncovered should be covered with *idhkhir* (a sweet smelling rush) or any other form of grass.

(5) If there is a shortage of shrouds and a large number of bodies, then it is permissible to shroud a number of them in a single shroud by sharing it between them and the one knowing most of the Qur'aan is placed first, i.e. closest to the Qiblah.

(6) It is not permissible to remove the clothes of the martyr which he died in, rather he is buried in them.

(7) It is recommended to shroud the martyr with a single cloth or more over his clothes.

(8) Whoever dies in *ihraam* is shrouded with the two sheets he was wearing when he died.

(9) A number of matters are recommended for the shroud:
    (a) That it be white,
    (b) That it comprises three cloths,
    (c) That one of them is a striped garment,[28]
    (d) That it be perfumed with incense fumes three times, this is only for those not in *ihraam*.

(10) It is not allowed to be extravagant with regard to the shroud, nor to increase upon the three cloths, since it is contrary to how Allaah's Messenger (ﷺ) was shrouded, not to mention being a waste of wealth.

(11) The woman is the same in that as the man, since there is no proof to make a distinction between them.

The Funeral Procession

(1) It is obligatory to carry the body and to follow the funeral procession. This is one of the rights of the Muslims upon the other Muslims.

(2) Following the funeral procession is of two degrees:
    (a) Following it from the home until the prayer is done.
    (b) Following it from the home until the burial is completed - and this is better.

---

[28] This does not contradict point (a), since it may be achieved in one of two ways, (i) That it is a striped garment and the predominant colour is white, or (ii) One of the garments may be striped and the other two white.

(3) Following the funeral procession is for the men and not the women due to the Prophet (ﷺ) having forbidden the women from following it.

(4) It is not allowed to accompany the funeral procession with that which conflicts with the *Sharee'ah*, for example, weeping loudly and carrying incense and the like.[29]

(5) It is obligatory to hasten with the funeral procession, without going faster than a quick walk.

(6) It is permissible to walk in front of it, or behind it,[30] or on the right, or on the left, as long as he is near to it, except for the rider who should ride behind.[31]

(7) It is permissible to ride without any dislike after the burial.

(8) As regards carrying the body upon a trolley, or in a funeral car,[32] and those in the funeral procession also travelling in vehicles, then that is not prescribed, since it is a custom of the unbelievers and it causes the purpose of following the funeral procession and carrying it, i.e. to reflect on the Hereafter, to be lost. Not to mention the fact that it is a cause of reduction in the number of people following the funeral procession and hoping to achieve reward through that.

(9) Standing up for the passage of a funeral procession was abrogated, so it is not to be done.

---

[29] This also includes the saying of the common people at that time, 'Declare Allaah's unity,' and other innovated *dhikrs*. Rather what is prescribed is silence, and to consider and reflect.

[30] That is better as occurs in some narrations.

[31] Whilst it is also better for him to walk.

[32] Except for necessity.

(10) It is recommended for the one who carried the deceased in the funeral procession to make wudoo', and it is not obligatory.

The Funeral Prayer

(1) Prayer over the deceased Muslim is *Fard Kifaayah* (i.e. it is obligatory that it be done by some, but not all of the people).

(2) Prayer is not obligatory[33] upon:
    (a) The child below the age of puberty,[34]
    (b) The martyr.

(3) Funeral prayer is also prescribed to be read over the following:
    (a) One who was executed as a prescribed punishment (*Hadd*).
    (b) The shameless sinner who commits sins and forbidden acts. However the people of excellence should not pray over them, as a punishment and as a deterrent for others.
    (c) The person who dies in debt, not leaving wealth to pay the debt, should be prayed over.
    (d) If someone was buried before the prayer was said over him,[35] then they can pray over him with him in the grave.[36]
    (e) If a person dies in a land where there is no one to pray over him, then a group of the Muslims should perform funeral prayers for him in their land (*Salatul-Ghaa'ib*).[37]

---

[33] It is however prescribed, but without being an obligation.

[34] Prayer is prescribed over them even if it was a miscarried foetus, as long as it has completed four months in the womb and then died. As for an embryo miscarried before that, then that is not the case.

[35] Or if only some of the people prayed over him then the others can do so here.

[36] The *imaam* being someone who did not pray over him previously.

[37] This is the situation when it is to be done, not unrestrictedly for anyone who dies in another land.

(4) It is forbidden to pray over, and to ask forgiveness for, and to invoke mercy upon the unbelievers and the hypocrites (*munaafiqoon*).[38]

(5) It is obligatory that the funeral prayer be said in congregation, the same as the other obligatory prayers. If however they were to pray it individually then they would have fulfilled the obligation of the prayer, but would have been sinful for their abandonment of the congregation, and Allaah knows best.

(6) The smallest number reported to constitute a congregation for it is three persons.

(7) The larger the congregation the better it is for the deceased.

(8) It is recommended that the congregation line themselves in three rows or more behind the *imaam*.

(9) If only one man can be found along with the imaam, them he should stand directly behind the imaam, and not stand right next to him as is the *Sunnah* for the rest of the prayers.[39]

(10) The ruler or his deputy, if present, has the most right to lead the prayer, and if he is not present then the one knowing the most Qur'aan has the most right. Then the order is as reported in the *Sunnah*.

(11) If there are a number of funerals, for men and women, all at once, then a single prayer may be said over them all, and the males, even if they are children, are placed nearest to the *imaam* and the females nearest the Qiblah.

---

38 They are to be known by their speaking against *Sharee'ah* rulings and their disproval of them and so on.

39 This shows the mistake of many people who, when they pray along with one other person, then the follower stands a little way behind the *imaam*!

(12) It is also permissible to pray a separate prayer over each of the funerals since that is the original principle.

(13) It is best that funeral prayer is held outside the mosque in a place prepared for funeral prayer. It is, however, permissible in the mosque, since both practices are established from the Prophet (ﷺ).

(14) It is not permissible to pray funeral prayer amongst the graves.[40]

(15) The *imaam* should stand behind the head of a deceased male and behind the middle of a deceased woman.

(16) He should say four *takbeers* over it, that being the most preferable, or five, up to a maximum of nine, all of this being established from the Prophet (ﷺ). Therefore what is best, is to sometimes do it one way and sometimes another.

(17) It is prescribed to raise the hands only with the first *takbeer.*

(18) Then he should place his right hand upon his left hand and put them on his chest.

(19) After the first *takbeer* he should recite Soorah al-Faatihah and another Soorah.[41]

(20) One should recite quietly.

---

[40] This does not contradict what occurs in point 3 (d), p.26, as will be clear to one who considers carefully.

[41] It is not reported that one should recite the opening supplication (*du'aa-ul-Istiftaah*) here as is the case with the usual prayers.

(21) Then the second *takbeer* should be said after which *salaat* should be sent upon the Prophet (ﷺ).[42]

(22) Then he should say the remaining *takbeers*, between which he should sincerely make supplication for the deceased.

(23) The supplication which he makes for the deceased should be from that which is established from the Prophet (ﷺ).[43]

(24) Supplication between the final *takbeer* and the *tasleem*[44] is prescribed.

---

[42] e.g. by ones saying, *Allaahumma salli 'alaa Muhammad wa...* etc, using any of the authentic wordings for sending *salaat* upon the Prophet (ﷺ) which can be found in 'The Prophet's (ﷺ) Prayer Described,' by Shaykh Muhammad Naasiruddeen Al-Albaani pp.70-73 (Al-Haneef Publications). **[Translator' note]**

[43] For example,

«اللهم عبدك وابن أمتك احتاج إلى رحمتك، وأنت غني عن عذابه،
إن كان محسناً فزد في حسناته، وإن كان سيئاً فتجاوز عن سيئاته»

(*Allaahumma 'abduka wabnu amatikahtaaja ilaa rahmatika, wa anta ghaniyyun 'an 'adhaabihi, in kaan muhsinan fazid fee hasanaatihi, wa in kaana sayyi'an fatajaawuza 'an sayyi'aatihi*)
'O Allaah, Your slave, son of Your female slave, in need of Your Mercy, and You are free from any need to punish him, if he was a doer of good then increase his good, and if he committed evil then pardon him.'

Translator's note: A further example of a supplication that is found in the *Sunnah* is:

«اللهُمَّ اغْفِرْ لِحَيِّنا ومَيِّتِنا، وشَاهِدِنا وغَائِبِنا، وصَغِيرنا وكبِيرنا، وذَكَرِنا وأنْثانا، اللهُمَّ
مَنْ أَحْيَيْتَهُ مِنّا فأَحْيِهِ على الإسْلامِ، ومَن تَوَفَّيْتَهُ مِنّا فَتَوَفَّهُ على الإيمانِ،
اللهُمَّ لا تَحْرِمْنا أَجْرَهُ، ولا تُضِلَّنا بعدَهُ».

(*Allaahum maghfirli hayyinaa wa mayyitinaa, wa shaahidinaa wa ghaa'ibinaa, wa sagheerinaa wa kabeerinaa, wa dhakarinaa wa unthaanaa, allaahumma man ahyaitahoo minnaa fa ahyihee 'alal islaami, wa man tawaffaitahoo minna fatawaffahoo 'alal eemaani, allaahumma laa tahrimnaa ajrahoo, walaa tudillanaa ba'dahoo*)
'O Allaah, forgive our living and our dead, those of us who are present and those who are absent, our young and or old, our males and our females, O Allaah, whoever amongst us You cause to live, then cause them to live upon Islaam, and whoever from us You cause to die then cause him to die upon *eemaan*. O Allaah, do not forbid us his reward, and do not cause us to go astray after him.'

[44] Saying, *As-Salaamu-'alaykum...*

(25) Then he should give two *tasleems* like the *tasleems* in the obligatory prayer. One on the right and the second on the left. It is also permissible to just give the first *tasleem*, since both of these ways are reported in the noble *Sunnah*.

(26) The *Sunnah* is that the *tasleem* in the funeral prayer is said quietly, the *imaam* and the followers being the same in that.

(27) It is not allowed to pray the funeral prayer in the times when prayer is forbidden[45] except out of necessity.

Burial and Related Matters

(1) Burial of the deceased is obligatory, even if he is an unbeliever.

(2) No Muslim is buried along with an unbeliever, nor an unbeliever along with a Muslim. Rather each must be buried in their own graveyard.

(3) The *Sunnah* is to bury the deceased in the graveyard,[46] except for the martyrs, since they should be buried at the place where they were martyred and not transferred to a graveyard.

(4) It is not permitted to bury the dead in the forbidden times[47] or at night, except when forced by circumstances, even if a lamp is then lowered into the grave in order to facilitate the burial.

(5) It is obligatory to make the grave deep and roomy and to do it well.

---

[45] i.e. when the sun is starting to rise, when the sun is at its highest point in the sky, and when it is setting.

[46] Which contains a proof to those who write in their will that they should be buried in a mosque, or a mausoleum or such place, and this is not permitted in Allaah's *Deen*.

[47] See footnote no. 45.

(6) There are two ways of making the grave, the first being the best:

(a) '*al-Lahd*,' A grave with a niche in the Qiblah side for the body.

(b) '*ash-Shaqq*,' A simple grave dug straight down.

(7) There is no harm in burying two people or more in a single grave when there is a need, the best of them being placed first.

(8) The deceased, even if a female, should be lowered into the grave by men and not women.

(9) The near relatives of the deceased have the most right to lower him into his grave.

(10) It is allowed for the husband to take charge of his wife's burial himself.

(11) It is a condition for the one who buries a woman that he should not have had sexual intercourse with his wife the previous night.

(12) The *Sunnah* is to enter the body from the foot of the grave.

(13) The body is placed in the grave on its right side with its face towards the Qiblah.

(14) The one who places him in the grave should say,

«بِسمِ اللهِ، وَعَلى سُنَّةِ رَسُولِ اللهِ ﷺ» .

(*Bismillaahi wa 'alaa sunnati* rasoolillaah*)

"With the name of Allaah and upon the *Sunnah* of Allaah's Messenger (ﷺ)."

---

* Or in another wording "...'*alaa millati rasoolillaah*"

(15) It is recommended for those around the grave to throw three handfuls of earth upon the grave, with both hands together after filling the grave.

(16) It is *Sunnah* after the burial to do the following:

(a) To make the grave stand above ground level by about a handspan and not level with the ground, so that it can be recognised as such and not mistreated.

(b) To make this protuberance above the ground convex.

(c) To mark it with a rock or the like so it can be recognised.

(d) To stand by the grave and supplicate that he be granted firmness and forgiveness, and to order those present to do this.[48]

(17) It is allowed to sit by the grave after burial with the intention of giving admonition about death and that which comes after it.[49]

(18) The practice of some, digging the grave before death is not recommended since the Prophet (ﷺ) did not do that, nor did the Companions, and a person does not know when he will die. If it is done with the intention of preparing for the death and to remember it, then that should rather be done by the performance of righteous actions and visiting graves! and not through actions which have been innovated in the *Deen*!

Giving Condolences to the Relatives and Advising them to Bear the Loss with Patience

(1) It is prescribed to encourage the relatives of the deceased to have patience and to await the promise of reward and to supplicate for the deceased.

---

[48] This is what is reported here. As regards the practice of the common people which is to address the deceased and advise him to recite the *Shahaadah* etc, then it is not reported in the authentic *Sunnah*. So be aware!

[49] See the *hadeeth* of Al-Baraa ibn 'Aazib, p.12.

(2) He should console them in a manner which he thinks will comfort them and relieve their grief and cause them to be content and to have patience, saying what is authentic from Allaah's Messenger (ﷺ)[50] if he knows and can recall it, but if not then whatever good words he can find to achieve the purpose, as long as it does not conflict with the *Sharee'ah*.

(3) The giving of condolences is not limited to three days, rather whenever there is benefit in giving condolences then it is done.

(4) Two matters are to be avoided even though they are common amongst the people:

> (a) Gathering in a particular place, such as the house, or the graveyard, or the mosque to receive condolences.
> (b) The family of the deceased preparing food for the guests who have come to give condolences.[51]

(5) Rather the *Sunnah* is that the neighbours and those close to the deceased should prepare sufficient food for the family of the deceased.

(6) It is recommended to stroke the head of the orphan and to treat him well and with kindness.

---

[50] For example,

$$ أَنَّ لِلهِ تَعَالَى مَا أَخَذَ وَلَهُ مَا أَعْطَى ، وَكُلُّ شَيْءٍ عِنْدَهُ بِأَجَلٍ مُسَمَّى ، $$
$$ فَلْتَصْبِرْ وَلْتَحْتَسِبْ $$

(Inna lillaahi ta'aala maa akhadha wa maa a'taa wa kullu shay'in 'indahu bi ajalin musammaa - faltasbir wal tahtasib)
"Indeed what Allaah took and what He gave was His, and everything has an appointed time with Him... so have patience and wait for reward."

[51] Like it are their return visits after three days, or a week, or forty days, the like of which has no basis in the *Sharee'ah*.

Actions which will Benefit the Deceased.

(1) A Muslim supplicating for him.

(2) The inheritor of the deceased carrying out any fast which the deceased had vowed to perform.

(3) The payment of his debts by anyone, whether an inheritor or not.[52]

(4) Any righteous action which the righteous child does, since the parents will receive the same as his reward, without anything being reduced from his reward.

(5) Any continuing good that he left behind and any continuing charity.

Visiting the Graves and Related Matters

(1) It is permissible to visit the graves in order to take admonition from them and in order to remind oneself of the Hereafter, but he must not say anything which will anger the Lord, the One far above and free of all defects and the Most High, such as calling in supplication upon the one buried in the grave, and seeking aid from him instead of from Allaah, the One far above and free of all defects and the Most High, or declaring him definitely pious, or that he is certainly in Paradise and so on.[53]

(2) Women are like men with regard to the recommendation of visiting the graves, with the condition that they do not mix with the men, nor wail and shriek, nor display themselves, nor fall into the other wicked actions which fill the graveyards these days.

---

[52] Refer to point 1(f), p.18.

[53] Such as the saying of some of them 'So and so the martyr (shaheed)', this is from the forbidden declaration of a persons being pious and it is why Al-Bukhaaree entitled a chapter of the Saheeh, 'Chapter: It is not to be said, 'So and so is a martyr.' Also refer to Fathul-Baaree (6/89).

(3) However it is not permitted for them to visit the graves often or repeatedly, since that may lead them to commit other actions prohibited in the *Sharee'ah* like what has just been mentioned.

(4) It is permissible to visit the grave of someone who died upon other than Islaam, but only in order to take heed and admonition.

(5) The purpose of visiting the graves is twofold:

> (a) So that the visitor may benefit from being reminded of death and the dead and that their final resting place can only be either Paradise or the Fire and that is the same for everyone.
> (b) So the deceased may be benefited by the visitors greeting him with 'salaam', and supplicating for him.[54]

(6) It is permissible to raise the hands while making supplication for the deceased when visiting the graves, since that is reported in the noble *Sunnah*, but without facing the graves. Rather it is the Qiblah that is to be faced when making supplication.

(7) If he visits the grave of an unbeliever then he may not greet him with *salaam*, nor may he supplicate for him, rather he should give him tidings of the Fire.

---

54 It is not prescribed to recite Soorah al-Faatihah or other *Soorahs* in the graveyard. Rather what is prescribed are the *du'aas* established from the Prophet (ﷺ) such as his saying (among others):

السَّلامُ على أَهلِ الدِّيارِ مِنَ المُؤمِنِينَ والمُسْلِمِينَ، ويَرْحَمُ اللهُ
المُسْتَقْدِمِينَ منكُمْ ومِنَّا والمُسْتَأْخِرِينَ، وإِنَّا إِنْ شاءَ اللهُ بكُمْ لاحِقُونَ

(As-salaamu 'alaa ahlid diyaari minal mu'mineena wal muslimeena, yarhamullaahul mustaqdimeen minnaa wal musta'khireen, wa innaa inshaa Allaahu bikum laahiqoon.)

"May Allaah send peace upon the people of this dwelling place, upon the Believers and the Muslims, and may Allaah forgive our earlier and later people, and we shall, if Allaah wills, be joining you."

(8) He should not walk amongst the graves of the Muslims wearing shoes, rather he should remove them.

(9) It is not prescribed to place sweet-smelling plants or roses upon the graves[55] since it was not the practice of the Predecessors (*Salaf*). If it were something good then they would have preceded us in it.

(10) The following actions are prohibited (*haraam*) with regards to graves:
  (a) Sacrificing animals there.
  (b) Raising graves high by adding to the earth that was dug out of it, keeping in mind the correct practice which has preceded.
  (c) Covering it with plaster or the like.[56]
  (d) Writing upon it.[57]
  (e) Building any structure upon it.
  (f) Sitting upon it.
  (g) Praying towards graves.
  (h) Praying at graves, even if one is not directly facing them.
  (i) Building mosques upon them.[58]
  (j) Taking them as places for recurring periodic visits at certain times.
  (k) Travelling to reach them.
  (l) Setting up lamps upon them.
  (m) Breaking the bones of the deceased Muslim.[59]

---

[55] Like it is the placing of palm-leaves upon the grave, and what is reported from Allaah's Messenger (ﷺ) about that is particular to him as a number of scholars have clearly stated.

[56] Unless it is necessary to preserve the grave.

[57] Unless it is needed simply to be able to identify the grave.

[58] This is not contradicted by the fact that at present the Prophet's (ﷺ) grave is within the mosque, since it was introduced into the mosque after the death of the Companions in Al-Madeenah by Al-Waleed ibn 'Abdul-Maalik in the year 88H, as explained fully by Shaykh Al-Albaanee in *Tahdheerus-Saajid*, pp 58-69. **[Translator's note]**

[59] As for the unbeliever then it is permissible since there is no honour and respect due to them.

(n) Exhuming the graves of Muslims unless it is for a purpose permitted by the *Sharee'ah*.

(11) It is permitted to exhume the graves of unbelievers since there is no honour or respect due to them.

Actions Conflicting with the *Sharee'ah* and Acts of Innovation (*Bid'ah*)

Many common people, not to mention some of those who claim to be *shaykhs*, fall into a large number of actions which are contrary to the *Sharee'ah* with regard to funerals and their regulations.[60] They think these actions are from the *Deen*, but they are not from it, either because they are contrary to the *Sunnah*, or because they do not occur in any text, or because they are from the customs of the unbelievers, or because the evidence for them is something which is not authentic, or because they are examples of exaggeration which has been forbidden, or due to other than this as is obvious to the well-grounded students of knowledge. So from these matters are:

(1) Reciting Soorah Yaa-Seen to the person who is dying.

(2) Turning the person who is dying to face the Qiblah.

(3) Entering cotton into the anus, throat and nose of the deceased.

(4) Abandonment of food by the relatives of the deceased until they have finished burying him.

(5) Allowing the beard to grow for a short while in mourning and then returning to shaving it.

---

[60] A number of them have already been mentioned in what has preceded.

(6) Announcing the death from the minarets.

(7) Saying when informed of the death, 'Read al-Faatihah for the soul of so and so.'

(8) The reciting of certain *dhikrs*, by the one who is washing the body of the deceased, upon washing each part.

(9) Raising the voice with *dhikr* whilst washing the deceased and whilst accompanying the funeral procession.

(10) Adorning the funeral procession.

(11) Placing a turban upon the bier.

(12) The belief of some of them that if the deceased was righteous then the body will be made light for those carrying it and will be carried more quickly and vice-versa.

(13) Conveying the body slowly in the funeral procession.

(14) Raising the voice with *dhikr* at the funeral and people holding conversations and the like.

(15) Lamenting and expressing one's grief when the deceased is brought before the Prayer, or after the Prayer and before the burial, or after the burial.

(16) Making it the practice to carry the deceased in a car and for the funeral procession to travel in cars.

(17) To pray funeral prayer for one who dies in another place, knowing that funeral prayer was said for him in that place.

(18) The standing of the *imaam* level with the middle of the man and the chest of the woman.

(19) The saying of the *imaam* or someone else after the Prayer in a loud voice, 'What do you testify concerning him?' and those present replying, 'He was one of the righteous'! and so on.

(20) Deliberately entering the body into the grave from the head of the grave.

(21) Laying out sand beneath the body without a need.

(22) Placing a pillow or the like beneath the head of the deceased in the grave.

(23) Sprinkling rose water upon the body of the deceased.

(24) Addressing the deceased with words such as, 'O so and so... when the two angels come then say... etc.'

(25) Giving condolences near the graves with the relatives standing in rows.

(26) Gathering for condolences in a particular place.

(27) Limiting condolences to three days.

(28) Giving condolences with the words, *'Azzamallaahu ajrakum'* (May Allaah grant you a great reward), thinking that it is the *Sunnah* whereas it is something which is not authentic.

(29) Preparation of food by the family of the deceased on various days.

(30) Making or buying pancakes on the seventh day after the death.

(31) Going out in the early morning to the grave of the one they buried on the previous day along with their relatives and companions.

(32) Remembering the deceased on the fortieth night after his death,[61] or after a year has passed.

(33) Digging the grave before death in preparation for it.

(34) Particularly visiting graves on the two days of 'eed.

(35) Particularly visiting graves on Mondays and Thursdays.

(36) Reciting Soorah al-Faatihah and Soorah Yaa-Seen over the graves.

(37) Sending greetings of *Salaam* to the Prophets via those who go to visit the graves.

(38) Seeking to grant the reward for actions of worship, such as Prayer and reciting the Qur'aan, as a gift for the deceased Muslims.

(39) Seeking to grant the reward for actions to the Prophet (ﷺ).

(40) Paying someone to recite the Qur'aan and to grant the reward to the deceased.

(41) Their saying that supplication made near to the graves of the Prophets and righteous is answered.

---

[61] 'Abdur-Razzaaq Nawfal says in *Al-Hayaatul-Ukhraa* p.156, 'This practice done after forty nights came from the Pharoahs who used to spend the first forty nights embalming and preparing the body and then travelling to the grave after which they celebrated the burial!'

(42) Adorning graves.

(43) Touching and kissing the grave of the Prophet (ﷺ).

(44) Performing *tawaaf* around the graves of the Prophets and the Pious.[62]

(45) Calling upon the deceased for removal of distress or requesting supplication from him.

(46) Elevating the grave and building a structure upon it.

(47) Inscribing the name of the deceased and the date of his death on the grave.

(48) Burying the deceased in the mosque or building a mosque over his grave.

(49) Travelling to visit the graves of the Prophets.

(50) Sending pieces of paper stating your needs to the grave of the Prophet (ﷺ).

(51) Their saying, 'There is no difference between the death of the Prophet (ﷺ) and his life with regards to his watching over his *Ummah* and knowing their condition and all of their affairs.'

This is the end of what I have been able to abridge with regard to funeral regulation in Islamic *Fiqh*, and all praise is for Allaah who guides to and grants what is correct.

---

[62] As is done by the ignorant in some parts of the Islamic world, for example in Egypt, and unfortunately there are those from the misguided *shaykhs* of innovation who declare that it is permissible for them.

Chapter 3

The Will as Prescribed in the *Sharee'ah*

The encouragement to write a will is found in the noble Prophetic *Sunnah*. He (ﷺ) said, "It is not fitting for any Muslim who has something to include in a will that he remains for two nights except that his will is written and kept with him."[63] Ibn 'Umar (*radiyallaahu 'anhumaa*) said, "No night has passed me by since I heard Allaah's Messenger (ﷺ) say that except that my will was with me."[64]

The person making a will should do the following:
(1) To include in the will those relatives who do not inherit from him.
(2) That he only bequeaths one third of his wealth or less in his will, it is not permissible to bequeath more than that.
(3) He should have as witnesses two just Muslims.
(4) As regards bequeathing in the will for those who inherit from him, then that is not allowed.
(5) It is also forbidden to use the will to cause harm and oppression, for example deliberately depriving some, or preferring some children to others, etc.
(6) Since a large number of people are overcome by innovation in the *Deen* these days, particularly with regard to funerals, then it is a duty upon the Muslim that he orders in his will that he should be prepared for burial and buried upon the *Sunnah*.

This is the text of a will as prescribed in the *Sharee'ah*:[65]

---

[63] Reported by Al-Bukhaaree, Muslim and others.

[64] Reported by Al-Bukhaaree, Muslim and others.

[65] *Riyaadul-Jannah*, pp 152-157, of Muhammad Mahdee Istanboolee, adapted.

In the name of Allaah, the Most Merciful, the Bestower of Mercy.

This is the will of _____ that he testifies that none has the right to be worshipped but Allaah alone, having no partner, and that Muhammad is His Slave and Messenger, and that Allaah will resurrect those in the graves. I advise my family to fear Allaah and to keep up ties of relationship, and that they obey Allaah and His Messenger. I enjoin upon you that which Ibraaheem enjoined upon his sons and as did Ya'qoob:

وَوَصَّىٰ بِهَآ إِبْرَٰهِـۧمُ بَنِيهِ وَيَعْقُوبُ يَـٰبَنِىَّ إِنَّ ٱللَّهَ ٱصْطَفَىٰ لَكُمُ ٱلدِّينَ فَلَا تَمُوتُنَّ إِلَّا وَأَنتُم مُّسْلِمُونَ ﴿١٣٢﴾

And this (submission to Allaah, Islaam) was enjoined by Ibraaheem upon his sons and by Ya'qoob, (saying), "O my sons! Allaah has chosen for you the (true) religion, then die not except in the Faith of Islam (as Muslims - Islamic Monotheism).

[Soorah al-Baqarah (2):132]

I enjoin upon you that which the Messenger of Allaah (ﷺ) enjoined upon his Ummah, "...The Prayer... the Prayer." And I hope that Allaah will guide you to acting in a manner that will lead to my comfort, merciful treatment and to my Lord being pleased with me. So it is upon you to implement my will as follows:

(1) That I should be attended when dying by some of the people of knowledge and piety, so that they remind me to have good thoughts about my Lord, and to hope for His mercy and forgiveness.

(2) That they remind me of the word of Tawheed (laa ilaaha illallaah) from time to time.

(3) When my soul departs then let them close my eyes and supplicate good for me and hasten to prepare me for the burial and to bury me according to the Sunnah of the Prophet (ﷺ).

(4) That raising the voice, wailing, lamenting, striking the cheeks and calling out with the calls of ignorance is to be forbidden.

(5) That encouraging me to say the 'shahaadah' after I have died be totally prevented.

(6) That henna should not be sprinkled in the grave, nor should any pillow or the like be placed beneath my head.

(7) That condolences should only be given upon the first meeting with the family of the deceased.

(8) That those things which have become common, reciting the Qur'aan over the dead during the funeral preparations, or on the day of Jumu'ah,

or after forty days, and other innovations, all this is to be prevented.

(9) Along with this I bequeath the following amounts of money _____ and _____ from my wealth to be given to the needy from those who are relatives, the orphans and the poor and I make this particular to those who act in accordance with the pure Sunnah.

I further bequeath the amount of _____ from my wealth to be placed in the care of _____ so as to be spent upon works for admonishment and guidance, and for the establishment of the rites and practices of the Sharee'ah, and I have left the decision as to when and where it is to be spent with _____.

I also give the following books to the students of knowledge _____.

I declare myself free before Allaah, the Most High, from every action, and every saying which conflicts with the way of the noble Messenger (ﷺ).

This is my will* which I have laid out.

---

* N.B. The will is not reported in the *Sunnah* with this particular wording, but we believe that it is what is closest, if Allaah wills, so even if a person does not stick to its wording yet he should stick to its meaning and content, and Allaah knows best.

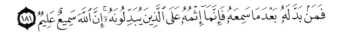

"Then whoever changes the bequest after hearing it, the sin shall be on those who make the change. Truly, Allaah is All-Hearer, All-Knower."

[Soorah al-Baqarah (2):181]

I ask Allaah that He guides me and all the Muslims and grants them that which is correct, a good end, and death upon the word 'La ilaaha illallah' (None has the right to be worshipped except Allaah).

Glorified be your Lord, the Lord of Honour and Power! (He is free) from what they attribute to Him! And peace be on the Messengers! And all praise and thanks be to Allaah, Lord of the *Aalameen* (mankind, jinn and all that exists).

Dated:.............   The year: ......H

Witness:...............................

Witness:...............................

Signature (Testator) of
the one leaving the will:.................

Conclusion

The compiler of this treatise 'Alee Hasan 'Alee 'Abdul-Hameed al-Halabee, may Allaah grant him and the Muslims a good end says: The abridgement of this quick work and additions made to it were completed in sittings on the days of Monday and Tuesday the 21st and 22nd of Muharram 1405, after the Hijrah of the Prophet (ﷺ).

I ask Allaah, the Most Great and Sublime, that He causes it to be of benefit to me and all the Muslims. Indeed He hears and responds, and our final call is that all praise is for Allaah, Lord of the worlds.

Glossary

Aayah (pl. Aayaat): The Sign of Allaah; a number of His Words occurring together in the Qur'aan.

Aayaat: See *Aayah*

Ahaadeeth: See *Hadeeth*

'Alaihis-salaam: "May Allaah, the One free of all defects, protect and preserve him." It is said after the name of a Prophet of Allaah or after the name of any angel.

Ansaar: "Helpers"; the Muslims of Madeenah who supported the Muslims who migrated from Makkah.

'Aqeedah: The principles and details of Belief.

Bid'ah: Innovation; anything introduced into the *Deen*, in order to seek Allaah's pleasure, not having a specific proof or basis in the *Deen*.

Companion: (Ar. Sahaabee) A Muslim who met the Prophet (ﷺ) and died as a Muslim.

Deen: The complete way of life revealed by Allaah; Islaam.

Dhikr: Remembrance of Allaah with the heart and tongue, and remembrance of what He has ordered and prohibited.

Du'aa: Invocation; supplication.

'Eed: A day of festival for the Muslims, there are two *'eeds* every year, one marking the end of Ramadaan and the other in the month of Dhul-Hijjah.

Fard Kifaayah: Collective obligation - if fulfilled by a part of the community then the rest are not obliged to fulfil it.

Fiqh: The understanding and application of the *Sharee'ah* from its sources.

Hadd: Boundary or limit between the *halaal* and the *haraam*; a prescribed punishment.

Hadeeth (pl. Ahaadeeth): Narration concerning the utterances of the Prophet (ﷺ), his actions or an attribute of his.

Haraam: Prohibited under the *Sharee'ah*.

Idhkhir: A special type of pleasantly scented grass found in the Hijaaz area of Arabia.

Ihraam: The state one is in while performing Hajj or 'Umrah; the dress worn while performing Hajj or 'Umrah.

'Illiyyoon: A high place in the seventh heaven where the records of the righteous are kept. From the root word *'uluww* signifying 'highness'.

Imaam: Leader; leader in Prayer, knowledge or *fiqh*; leader of a state.

Istirjaa': Saying, "*Inna lillaahi wa inaa ilaihi raaji'oon.*" See p.19.

Jaahiliyyah: Ignorance; the period before the advent of the Prophet (ﷺ).

Janaabah: A state requiring that one purifies oneself by taking a bath e.g. after sexual intercourse.

Mustahabb: Recommended; one who does a *mustahabb* action is rewarded, but one who leaves it is not punished.

Niyaahah: Wailing and shrieking for the deceased, tearing at ones clothes and hair, and other similar forbidden actions.

Qiblah: The direction ones faces during Prayer (i.e. towards Makkah).

Radiyallaahu 'anhu/'anhaa/'anhum/'anhumaa: May Allaah be pleased with him/her/them/both of them.

Sadaqah: Voluntary charity.

Salaat: Prescribed Prayer (e.g. the five obligatory prayers); prayers upon the Prophet (ﷺ).

Salaf: Predecessors; the early Muslims; the Muslims of the first three generations: the *Companions*, the *Successors* and their successors.

Shahaadah: To bear witness (that none has the right to be worshipped except Allaah); Martyrdom.

Sharee'ah: The Divine code of Law.

Shaykh: Scholar.

Sijjeen: The place where the records of the evil doers are kept. Comes from the root *sijn* which means prison. See also Qur'aan Soorah al-Mutaffifeen (83):7-9.

Soorah: A Chapter of the Qur'aan.

Sunnah: In its broadest sense the entire Religion which the Prophet (ﷺ) came with, i.e. all matters of beliefs, rulings, manners and actions which were conveyed by the *Companions*. It also includes those matters which the Prophet (ﷺ) established by his sayings, actions and tacit approvals. It can also include the physical attributes of the Prophet (ﷺ).

Takbeer: "Allaahu akbar."

Tasleem: "Assalaamu 'alaykum..."

Tawaaf: Circling the Ka'bah seven times as an act of worship (many ignorant people have begun to circle graves and other such places, this is completely forbidden, being a flagrant violation of the Qur'an and *Sunnah*).

Wudoo': Ablution; the ritual washing before Prayer and certain other acts of worship.

Zakaat: Charity that is obligatory on anyone who has wealth over and above a certain limit over which a year has passed.